Central Intelligence: Origin and Evolution

Editor
Michael Warner

CIA History Staff
Center for the Study of Intelligence
Central Intelligence Agency
Washington, DC
2001

Foreword

In May 2001, President George W. Bush directed that the Director of Central Intelligence commission the first in-depth study of the nation's Intelligence Community in three decades. The panels appointed by DCI George Tenet will soon provide him, and the President, with their findings about the shape of the changing international order and the ability of the Intelligence Community to respond to the national security challenges and opportunities of the 21st Century.

After the panels present their findings, the Central Intelligence Agency's Center for the Study of Intelligence, in conjunction with the Institute for the Study of Diplomacy at Georgetown University, intends to sponsor a conference to examine the transition required of the Intelligence Community. Panelists and attendees will strive to gain a clearer idea of what in our new era constitutes "intelligence" to policymakers, diplomats, commanders, and law enforcement officials. Conferees will also examine the ways in which the components of the Intelligence Community have adapted since the Cold War and the areas where change is still needed.

What is the future of "central" intelligence? The creators of the CIA in Congress and the White House believed that the reforms accomplished by the National Security Act of 1947 would minimize problems that had lulled the nation's vigilance before Pearl Harbor. The centralization implied in the Truman administration's directives and the National Security Act never fully occurred, however, mainly because of the limits on DCI powers codified in that very Act. As the Cold War recedes into the past and a new world order emerges, it is important to understand why intelligence was centralized in the form it was, and to explore differing views about its future. The assault on New York's World Trade Center towers and the Pentagon in Washington bring this question into very sharp focus.

Michael Warner of the CIA History Staff in the Center for the Study of Intelligence has compiled a set of key declassified laws, executive orders, NSCIDs, DCIDs, and policy documents guiding the role and growth of the central intelligence function from 1945 to 2000. As a member of the staff that assisted in the preparation of the NSPD-5 report, Dr. Warner observed at close hand the ways in which the assumptions and charters of the Intelligence Community have endured over the decades and the fates of various attempts to modify them. His draft introduction to this volume informed the work of the NSPD-5 staff, and I commend it to students of the Intelligence Community for its scope and its insight.

Admiral David E. Jeremiah,
United States Navy (Retired)
September 2001

CONTENTS

Historical Perspective

"...what have appeared to be the most striking successes have often, if they are not rightly used, brought the most overwhelming disasters in their train, and conversely the most terrible calamities have, if bravely endured, actually turned out to benefit the sufferers."

Polybius, *The Rise of the Roman Empire,*
Book III, 7

The explosions at Pearl Harbor still echoed in Washington when President Harry Truman and Congressional leaders passed the National Security Act of 1947. A joint Congressional investigation just a year earlier had concluded that the Pearl Harbor disaster illustrated America's need for a unified command structure and a better intelligence system.[1] Indeed, the President and many of his aides rightly believed that the surprise attack could have been blunted if the various commanders and departments had coordinated their actions and shared their intelligence. With that thought in mind, the creators of the National Security Act attempted to implement the principles of unity of command and unity of intelligence, fashioning a National Security Council, a Secretary of Defense, a statutory Joint Chiefs of Staff and a Central Intelligence Agency.

In almost the next breath, however, the National Security Act made important concessions to the traditional American distrust of large military establishments and centralized power. The Act (among other qualifications) ensured that the Joint Chiefs would not become a Prussian-style "General Staff," created an independent air force, and insisted that the new Central Intelligence Agency (CIA) would have no law enforcement powers. The Act also decreed that the intelligence divisions in the armed services and the civilian departments (what came to be called the "Intelligence Community") would remain independent of the CIA.

Since 1947 Directors of Central Intelligence (DCIs) have served within the bounds of this ambiguous mandate. They have had the responsibility of coordinating national intelligence collection and production without a full measure of the authority they needed to do so. Many Presidents and Congresses—not to mention DCIs—have expressed their frustration with this ambiguity and have assumed that the solution to the dilemmas it created lay in concentrating more power in the office of the Director of Central Intelligence. This centralizing impulse has prompted various reforms to increase the Director's ability to lead the Intelligence Community. For years these attempts were made by the National Security Council (NSC) through a series of NSC Intelligence

---

[1] Joint Committee on the Investigation of the Pearl Harbor Attack, "Investigation of the Pearl Harbor Attack," 79th Congress, 2nd Session, 1946, pp. 252-253. (U)

Directives. In the wake of "the time of troubles" for the Intelligence Community in the mid-1970s—marked by investigations into questions about excesses and accountability—three Presidents issued successive executive orders aimed at one goal: rationalizing American intelligence and increasing the DCI's power. Since the end of the Cold War, Congress itself has taken up the task, repeatedly amending the intelligence sections of the National Security Act.

The various regulations and amendments, however, have not fundamentally altered the "federalist" intelligence structure created in 1947. Strong centrifugal forces remain, particularly in the Department of Defense and its Congressional allies. Indeed, the case for centralization seems to be countered by historical illustrations of the perils of excessive concentration. In actual practice, the successful end to the Cold War and the lack of any national intelligence disasters since then seem to militate in favor of keeping the existing structure until some crisis proves it to be in dire need of repair.

Reform After World War II

The Agency began its statutory existence in September 1947—its creation ratifying, in a sense, a series of decisions taken soon after the end of the Second World War.[2] That conflict ended in the summer of 1945 with Washington decisionmakers in broad agreement that the United States needed to reform the intelligence establishment that had grown so rapidly and haphazardly during the national emergency. Nevertheless, when President Truman dissolved the wartime Office of Strategic Services (OSS) in September 1945 he had no clear plan for constructing the peacetime intelligence structure that he and his advisers believed they needed in an atomic age. President Truman wanted the reforms to be part and parcel of the "unification" of the armed services, but the overhaul of the military that the President wanted would take time to push through Congress.[3] In the interim, he created a Central Intelligence Group (CIG) to screen his incoming cables and supervise activities left over from the former OSS.

In early 1946, the White House authorized CIG to evaluate intelligence from all parts of the government, and to absorb the remnants of OSS's espionage and counterintelligence operations.[4] Initially these disparate components of the new CIG

---

[2] Shorthand reference to "the Agency" is commonly used, and is used herein, as synonymous with CIA. "Community" has long been used, and is herein, to denote the totality of US executive branch organizations that produce and provide foreign intelligence to US policymakers and military commanders.

[3] "Text of the President's Message to Congress Asking Unification of the Army and Navy," *New York Times*, 20 December 1945, p. 14.

[4] President Truman's 22 January 1946 directive establishing CIG is reprinted in US Department of State, *Foreign Relations of the United States*, 1945-1950, *Emergence of the Intelligence Establishment* (Washington, DC: United States Government Printing Office, 1996) [hereafter cited as *FRUS*], pp. 178-179. The first DCI, Sidney Souers, recalled in 1954 that he had been part of the collective effort (leading to CIG's establishment) to create "a central intelligence agency" that would ensure that national security policymakers "all would get the same intelligence—in contrast to the system that had prevailed, where the OSS would give one bit of intelligence to the President and not any to the secretaries of the military departments and the State Department, who had some responsibility to advise the President." Quoted in

shared little in common except an interest in foreign secrets and a sense that both strategic warning and clandestine activities abroad required "central" coordination. Indeed, these two missions came together in CIG almost by accident. Under the first two Directors of Central Intelligence, however, CIG and the Truman administration came to realize how strategic warning and clandestine activities complemented one another.

Meanwhile, the military "unification" issue overshadowed intelligence reform in Congressional and White House deliberations. In mid-1946 President Truman called again on Congress to unify the armed services. That April, the Senate's Military Affairs committee had approved a unification bill that provided for a central intelligence agency, but the draft legislation had snagged in the hostile Naval Affairs committee.[5] Perhaps with that bill in mind, Secretary of War Robert Patterson and Secretary of the Navy James Forrestal in May agreed among themselves that a defense reorganization bill should also provide for a central intelligence agency. President Truman the following month sent Congress the result of the Secretaries' accord (with modifications of his own), repeating his call for lawmakers to send him a unification bill to sign.[6]

The administration's judgment that a central intelligence agency was needed soon firmed into a consensus that the new Central Intelligence Group ought to form the basis of this new intelligence agency. Indeed, CIG continued to accrue missions and capabilities. Oversight of the CIG was performed by a committee called the National Intelligence Authority (NIA), comprising the Secretaries of State, War, and Navy, joined by the President's chief military adviser, Admiral William Leahy. National Intelligence Authority Directive 5, issued on 8 July 1946, provided the DCI with the basic implementation plan for the broad scope of powers envisioned in President Truman's charter for CIG. Indeed, it was NIAD-5 that created the real difference between OSS— an operations office with a sophisticated analytical capability—and CIG, a truly (albeit fledgling) national intelligence service authorized to perform strategic analysis and to conduct, coordinate and control clandestine activities abroad.

NIAD-5 represented perhaps the most expansive charter ever granted to a Director of Central Intelligence. It allowed CIG to "centralize" research and analysis in "fields of national security intelligence that are not being presently performed or are not being adequately performed."[7] NIAD-5 also directed the DCI to coordinate all US foreign intelligence activities "to ensure that the over-all policies and objectives established by this Authority are properly implemented and executed." The National Intelligence Authority through this directive ordered the DCI to conduct "all organized Federal espionage and counter-espionage operations outside the United States and its

---

Ralph E. Weber, ed., *Spymasters: Ten CIA Officers in Their Own Words* (Wilmington, DE: Scholarly Resources, 1999), p. 3.

[5] David F. Rudgers, *Creating the Secret State: The Origins of the Central Intelligence Agency, 1943-1947* (Lawrence, KS: University of Kansas Press, 2000), p. 107.

[6] Anthony Leviero, "Truman Offers Congress 12-Point Program to Unify Armed Services of Nation," *New York Times*, 16 June 1946. For the Patterson-Forrestal accord in May 1946, see Walter Millis, ed., *The Forrestal Diaries* (New York: Viking, 1951), p. 163.

[7] National Intelligence Authority Directive number 5, 8 July 1946, reprinted in *FRUS*, pp. 391-392.

possessions for the collection of foreign intelligence information required for the national security."

In NIAD-5, the National Intelligence Authority determined that many foreign intelligence missions could be "more efficiently accomplished centrally" and gave CIG he authority to accomplish them. This in effect elevated CIG to the status of being the primary foreign intelligence arm of the US government. This mandate did not, however, give CIG the controlling role in intelligence analysis that DCI Hoyt Vandenberg had sought. The NIA's authorization was carefully phrased to allay fears that the DCI would take control of departmental intelligence offices; the Cabinet departments were not about to subordinate their own limited analytical capabilities to an upstart organization. In addition, NIAD-5 did not force a consolidation of clandestine activities under CIG control. Indeed, the Army defended the independence of its Intelligence Division's own collection operations by arguing that NIAD-5 gave CIG control only over "organized" foreign intelligence operations.

National Security Act of 1947

Congress initially paid scant attention to the new Central Intelligence Group. Indeed, CIG had been established with no appropriations and authority of its own precisely to keep it beneath Congressional scrutiny. As CIG gained new authority in 1946 and the White House gained confidence in its potential, however, a consensus emerged in Congress that postwar military reforms would not be complete without a simultaneous modernization of American intelligence capabilities.

The budding consensus even survived the death of the Truman administration's cherished unification bill in 1946. Ironically, prospects for unification only brightened when the opposition Republicans subsequently swept into control of the Congress in that year's elections, taking over the committee chairmanships and displacing powerful Democrats who had made themselves (in Harry Truman's words) "the principal stumbling blocks to unification."[8] With the President's goal of military modernization suddenly in sight, the White House firmly told DCI Vandenberg that enabling legislation for CIG would remain a small part of the defense reform bill then being re-drafted by the President's aides, and that the intelligence section would be kept as brief as possible in order to ensure that none of its details hampered the prospects for unification. [9]

---

[8] Harry S Truman, *Memoirs*, Volume II, *Years of Trial and Hope* (Garden City, NY, Doubleday, 1956), pp. 46-47.

[9] Admiral Forrest Sherman, a member of the White House team that drafted the bill, later told the House Committee on Expenditures that he and his colleagues feared that a detailed CIA section would prompt Congress to seek similar levels of detail in the armed services' sections of the bill, forcing a re-opening of the drafting process and possibly encumbering the draft with controversial specifics. See Lyle Miller's declassified draft, "Legislative History of the Central Intelligence Agency—National Security Act of 1947," Central Intelligence Agency (Office of Legislative Council), 25 July 1967, p. 72.

This tactic almost backfired. When President Truman sent his new bill forward in February 1947, the brevity of its intelligence provisions had the effect of attracting—not deflecting—Congressional scrutiny. Members of Congress eventually debated almost every word of the intelligence section, and made various adjustments. Ultimately, however, Congress passed what was essentially the White House's draft with important sections transferred (and clarified in the process) from Truman's 22 January 1946 directive establishing CIG—thus ratifying the major provisions of that directive. Thus the Central Intelligence Agency would be an independent agency under the supervision of the National Security Council; it would conduct both analysis and clandestine activities, but would have no policymaking role and no law enforcement powers; its Director would be confirmed by the Senate and could be either a civilian or a military officer.

What did Congress believe the new CIA would do? Testimony and debates over the draft bill unmistakably show that the lawmakers above all wanted CIA to provide the proposed National Security Council—the new organization that would coordinate and guide American foreign and defense policies—with the best possible information on developments abroad. Members of Congress described the information they expected CIA to provide as "full, accurate, and skillfully analyzed"; "coordinated, adequate" and "sound." Senior military commanders testifying on the bill's behalf used similar adjectives, saying the CIA's information should be "authenticated and evaluated"; "correct" and based on "complete coverage." When CIA provided such information, it was believed, the NSC would be able to assess accurately the relative strengths and weaknesses of America's overseas posture and adjust policies accordingly.[10]

Congress guaranteed CIA's independence and its access to departmental files in order to give it the best chance to produce authoritative information for the nation's policymakers. CIA was to stand outside the policymaking departments of the government, the better to "correlate and evaluate intelligence relating to the national security."[11] Although other departments and agencies would continue to handle intelligence of national importance, the Agency was the only entity specifically charged by the Act with the duty of producing it. To assist in the performance of this duty, the DCI had the right to "inspect" all foreign intelligence held by other agencies, as well as the right to disseminate it as appropriate. If the DCI happened to be a military officer, then he was to be outside the chain of command of his home service; this would help him resist any temptation to shade his reports to please his superiors.[12] Finally, the Agency was to provide for the US Government such "services of common concern" that the NSC would determine could more efficiently be conducted "centrally." In practice, this meant

---

[10] Quoted in Miller, "Legislative History," pp. 40, 45, 47, 48, 50.

[11] Sec. 102(d)3. The phrase came from President Truman's 22 January 1946 directive establishing CIG; see *FRUS*, p 178. The original pages of the intelligence section of the National Security Act of 1947 are reproduced in Michael Warner, ed., *The CIA under Harry Truman* (Washington: Central Intelligence Agency, 1994), pp. 131-135.

[12] The Act was amended in 1953 to provide for a Deputy Director of Central Intelligence (DDCI) with the stipulation (since removed) that the positions of DCI and DDCI must not "be occupied simultaneously by commissioned officers of the armed services, whether in an active or retired status."

espionage and other clandestine activities, as well as the collection of valuable information from open sources and American citizens.

Having approved the placement of these authorities and activities under one head, Congress in 1947 expected that CIA would provide the best possible intelligence and would coordinate clandestine operations abroad. Congress also implicitly assumed that the executive branch would manage CIA and the Intelligence Community with these purposes in mind.[13] After fixing this course in the statute books, Congress stepped back and left the White House and CIA to meet these expectations. This was how Congress resolved the apparent contradiction of creating "central intelligence" that was not centrally controlled. The institution of central intelligence would henceforth steer between the two poles of centralization and departmental autonomy.

Not Only National But Central

Congress passed the National Security Act on 26 July 1947 and President Truman immediately signed it into law. The act gave America something new in the annals of intelligence history; no other nation had structured its foreign intelligence establishment in quite the same way. CIA would be an independent, central agency, but not a controlling one; it would both rival and complement the efforts of the departmental intelligence organizations.[14] This prescription of coordination without control guaranteed friction and duplication of intelligence efforts as the CIA and the departmental agencies pursued common targets, but it also fostered a potentially healthy competition of views and abilities.

The National Security Council guided the Intelligence Community by means of a series of directives dubbed NSCIDs (the acronym stands for National Security Council Intelligence Directive). The original NSCIDs were issued in the months after the passage of the National Security Act. Foremost was NSCID 1, titled "Duties and

---

[13] Ludwell Montague believed the term "Intelligence Community" made its earliest documented appearance in the minutes of a 1952 meeting of the Intelligence Advisory Committee. For the sake of consistency the term Intelligence Community is used throughout this essay, even though the size and composition of the community has changed and now includes several large entities that did not exist when the National Security Act was passed in 1947. For example, of today's 13 intelligence organizations in the community, the National Security Agency, the Defense Intelligence Agency, the National Reconnaissance Office and the National Imagery and Mapping Agency are among the eight intelligence organizations that come under the Department of Defense. The only independent agency (that is, not part of a policy department) is CIA. For the 1952 usage of the term, see Ludwell Lee Montague, *General Walter Bedell Smith as Director of Central Intelligence: October 1950—February 1953* (University Park, PA: Pennsylvania State University Press, 1992), p. 74.

[14] At the time the Act went into effect, the intelligence agencies of the US government comprised the Central Intelligence Agency, the Federal Bureau of Investigation, the Office of Intelligence Research (State), the Intelligence Division (Army), the Office of Naval Intelligence, the Directorate of Intelligence (Air Force), and associated military signals intelligence offices, principally the Army Security Agency and the Navy's OP-20-G.

Responsibilities," which replaced NIAD-5 and established the basic responsibilities of the DCI and the interagency workings of the Intelligence Community.[15]

NSCID 1 did not re-write NIAD-5, but instead started afresh in the light of the debate over the National Security Act and the experience recently gained by the new CIA. Where the earlier document had authorized the DCI to coordinate "all Federal foreign intelligence activities" and sketched the initial outlines of his powers, NSCID 1 had to work within the lines already drawn by Congress and precedent. The Director who emerged from NSCID 1 was more circumscribed in his role and authority than previously. He was now to "make such surveys and inspections" as he needed in giving the NSC his "recommendations for the coordination of intelligence activities." Nonetheless, the DCI was—in keeping with Congress' implicit intent in the National Security Act—a substantial presence in the intelligence establishment. NSCID 1 gave the DCI an advisory committee comprising the heads of the departmental intelligence offices, and told him to "produce" intelligence (but to avoid duplicating departmental functions in doing so). The type of intelligence expected of him and his Agency was "national intelligence," a new term for the information that the National Security Act called "intelligence relating to the national security."[16] The DCI was also to perform for the benefit of the existing agencies such "services of common concern" as the NSC deemed could best be provided centrally. The NSC left the particulars of these responsibilities to be specified in accompanying NSCIDs (which eventually numbered 2 through 15 by the end of the Truman administration in 1953).[17]

Under this regime, DCIs were faced with contradictory mandates: they *could* coordinate intelligence, but they *must not* control it. Since the prohibitions in the statute and the NSCIDs were so much clearer than the permissions, every DCI naturally tended to steer on the side of looser rather than tighter oversight of common Intelligence Community issues. Because of this tendency to emphasize coordination instead of control, CIA never quite became the integrator of US intelligence that its presidential and congressional parents had envisioned. The DCI never became the manager of the Intelligence Community, his Agency never won the power to "inspect" the departments'

---

[15] All versions of NSCID 1 have been declassified and are available at the National Archives and Records Administration, Record Group 263 (CIA), NN3-263-91-004, box 4, HS/HC-500.

[16] NSCID 3 (13 January 1948) defined national intelligence as "integrated departmental intelligence that covers the broad aspects of national policy and national security, is of concern to more than one Department or Agency, and transcends the exclusive competence of a single Department or Agency or the Military Establishment." Its opposite was "departmental" intelligence, which NSCID 3 defined as intelligence needed by a department or agency "to execute its mission and discharge its lawful responsibilities;" see *FRUS*, p. 1109. Executive Order 11905 in 1976 retained "national intelligence" but changed its opposite to a phrase used in President Nixon's 1971 letter, "tactical intelligence" (which the executive order did not further define, apart from saying that the DCI shall not have responsibility for it). E.O. 11905 also added the overarching term "foreign intelligence," defining it as information "on the capabilities, intentions, and activities of foreign powers, organizations or their agents."

[17] It bears noting that the NSCIDs endorsed the NIA's 1946 assignment of the two main missions (strategic warning and the coordination of clandestine activities abroad) to the DCI and his Central Intelligence Group. In particular, NSCID 5 (12 December 1947) reaffirmed NIAD-5 in directing that the DCI "shall conduct all organized Federal espionage operations outside the United States...except for certain agreed activities by other Departments and Agencies." See *FRUS*, p. 1106.

operational plans or to extract community-wide consensus on disputed analytical issues, and CIA never had authority over all clandestine operations of the US Government.

Revisions and Oversight

This federalized intelligence structure did not satisfy the White House. Indeed, presidents from Dwight Eisenhower through Richard Nixon sought to adjust the NSCIDs to improve the functioning of the Intelligence Community, primarily by pushing successive DCIs to exert more control over common community issues and programs. President Eisenhower paid particular attention to this issue, approving in 1958 the first major revisions of NSCID 1. The September 1958 version of the revised directive added a preamble stressing the need for efficiency across the entire national intelligence effort, and began its first section by declaring "The Director of Central Intelligence shall coordinate the foreign intelligence activities of the United States...."

The September 1958 version of NSCID 1 also added a section on "community responsibilities" that listed the duties of the DCI to foster an efficient Intelligence Community and to ensure the quality of the intelligence information available to the US Government. It also emphasized to the existing departments and agencies their responsibilities to assist the DCI in these tasks. To this end, the new NSCID 1 created the United States Intelligence Board (USIB), a panel chaired by the DCI—with the Deputy Director of Central Intelligence (the DDCI) representing CIA—to coordinate a range of cooperative activities through a network of interagency committees. USIB soon built a sophisticated set of procedures, prompting former CIA Executive Director Lyman Kirkpatrick in 1973 to declare that "the USIB structure provides the community with probably the broadest and most comprehensive coordinating mechanism in the history of any nation's intelligence activities."[18]

In 1971 President Nixon turned to the topic of intelligence reform and issued a directive that precipitated the first major revision of NSCID 1 in over a decade. In the spirit of President Eisenhower's earlier initiatives, Nixon authorized a full-dress study of Intelligence Community cooperation, with an emphasis on cutting its costs and increasing its effectiveness. A committee headed by James Schlesinger of the Office of Management and Budget recommended major reforms, among them a greater role for the DCI in managing the Intelligence Community. President Nixon directed the adoption of many of these recommendations in a 5 November 1971 letter to the cabinet secretaries and senior policymakers who oversaw the community's far-flung components.[19] The NSC issued a revised NSCID 1 in February 1972 to disseminate the new guidance to the community.

---

[18] Lyman B. Kirkpatrick, Jr., *The US Intelligence Community: Foreign Policy and Domestic Activities* (New York: Hill & Wang, 1973), p. 39.

[19] Richard Nixon to the Secretary of State et al., "Organization and Management of the US Foreign Intelligence Community," 5 November 1971.

The new version retained much of the earlier text, while adding that the DCI had "four major responsibilities." He was to plan and review all intelligence activities and spending, submitting annually to the White House the community's overall "program/budget"; to produce national intelligence for the President and policymakers; to chair all community-wide advisory panels, and to establish intelligence requirements and priorities. In addition, the 1972 NSCID 1 established several objectives to guide the DCI in discharging these responsibilities. He was to seek the attainment of greater efficiency, better and more timely intelligence; and, perhaps most of all, "authoritative and responsible leadership for the community." The provision for DCI authority (albeit limited) over the Intelligence Community budget was new and significant; henceforth all subsequent directives governing the community would place at least one of the DCI's hands on the collective purse strings.

The years that followed the issuance of the 1972 version of NSCID 1 witnessed dramatic changes in the policy dynamic surrounding the Intelligence Community. For several reasons—many of them related to the Vietnam War and the Watergate scandal, but including Agency misdeeds under earlier administrations as well—Congress began to impose itself directly on CIA and other parts of the Intelligence Community in the mid-1970s. The White House responded to the new mood in Congress by acting to protect what it defended as the exclusive prerogatives of the executive branch. Republican and Democratic Presidents had long been content to delegate the chore of overseeing the community to the National Security Council, but President Gerald Ford, concerned that Congress would re-write the statutes undergirding the Intelligence Community, intervened with an executive order that supplanted the earlier NSCIDs.

Executive Order 11905 (18 February 1976) retained much of the language of the 1972 NSCID 1, but added much else as well. Most prominently, it established a lengthy list of restrictions on intelligence activities, which ran the gamut from a prohibition on the perusal of federal tax returns to a ban on "political assassination." E.O. 11905 also revisited the traditional ground covered by the now-obsolete NSCID 1 series, assigning "duties and responsibilities" to the DCI and the various members of the Intelligence Community.

President Ford's executive order did not diverge noticeably, however, from the earlier listings of the DCI's duties. These were now to be: acting as "executive head of the CIA and Intelligence Community staff;" preparing the community's budget, requirements and priorities; serving as "primary adviser on foreign intelligence," and implementing "special activities" (i.e., covert action). Indeed, E.O. 11905 encouraged the DCI to devote more energy to "the supervision and direction of the Intelligence Community." In this spirit, it revived an Eisenhower administration idea and urged the DCI to delegate "the day-to-day operation" of CIA to his Deputy Director for Central Intelligence.

President Jimmy Carter superseded E.O. 11905 with his own Executive Order 12036 barely two years later. The new order retained basically the same (albeit re-ordered) list of duties for the DCI in his dual role as manager of the Intelligence

Community and head of CIA. It also revamped the old United States Intelligence Board, expanding the list of topics on which it was to advise the DCI and renaming it the National Foreign Intelligence Board (NFIB). Where E.O. 12036 differed from preceding directives was in tasking the DCI to oversee the Intelligence Community budget. President Ford's executive order had created a three-member committee, chaired by the DCI, to prepare the budget and, when necessary, to reprogram funding.[20] Under the new provisions of E.O. 12036, however, the DCI now had "full and exclusive responsibility for approval of the National Foreign Intelligence Program budget." These combined powers were somewhat less sweeping than under E.O. 11905, but more concentrated in now being vested in the DCI alone. He would issue guidance to the community for program and budget development, evaluate the submissions of the various agencies, justify them before Congress, monitor implementation, and he could (after due consultation) reprogram funds.

President Ronald Reagan in his turn replaced the Carter directive with Executive Order 12333 (4 December 1981), which remains in effect today. The new order deleted provisions for the NFIB and other boards, allowing the DCI to arrange interagency advisory panels as he needed (DCI William Casey quickly reinstated the NFIB on his own authority). This was, however, almost the only enhancement of the DCI's power in an executive order that otherwise stepped back slightly from the centralization decreed by President Carter. Specifically, E.O. 12333 diluted DCI authority over the National Foreign Intelligence Program budget that E.O. 12036 had briefly strengthened. Where Carter had explicitly made the DCI the manager of the NFIP budgeting process, Reagan instead outlined a leading role for the DCI in developing the budget, reviewing requests for the reprogramming of funds and monitoring implementation. The change was not dramatic, but it was significant.

Management of the Intelligence Community by executive order during this period did not forestall increased Congressional oversight. In the 1970s both houses of Congress had created permanent intelligence oversight committees and passed legislation to tighten control of covert action. With the renewed polarization of foreign policy debates in the 1980s, both Republican and Democratic officials and lawmakers sought to "protect" intelligence from allegedly unprincipled forces that might somehow co-opt and abuse it to the detriment of the community and the nation's security. Responding to these concerns, Congress further toughened the new regulatory, oversight, and accountability regime to check the powers and potential for abuses at CIA and other agencies. Congress ensured permanence for these changes by codifying them as amendments to law, particularly to the National Security Act of 1947.

By the late 1980s, Congress's increased oversight role (and its new appetite for finished intelligence) prompted then-DDCI Robert Gates to comment publicly that CIA "now finds itself in a remarkable position, involuntarily poised nearly equidistant

---

[20] The panel had been created by E.O. 11905, which titled it the "Committee on Foreign Intelligence"; it comprised the DCI (chairman), the Deputy Secretary of Defense for Intelligence, and the Deputy Assistant to the President for National Security Affairs.

between the executive and legislative branches."[21] Not until the 1990s, however, did these changes significantly affect the "duties and responsibilities" of the DCI and the Intelligence Community.

Into a New Era

For the duration of the Cold War, the White House kept nudging successive Directors of Central Intelligence to do more to lead the Intelligence Community. DCIs more or less tried to comply. The statutory and institutional obstacles to centralization, however, proved daunting. Each DCI held budgetary and administrative sway only over the Central Intelligence Agency; the much larger budgets and staffs of the intelligence agencies in the Department of Defense (and their smaller cousins in other departments) remained firmly under cabinet-level officials who saw no reason to cede power to a DCI. Faced with this reality, DCIs had tended to let their community coordination duties suffer and to concentrate on the management of the CIA. Congress had intended a different course, however, and in the 1990s the legislative branch began its own campaign to encourage greater coordination in the Intelligence Community.

The end of the Cold War saw a subtle shift in Congressional attitudes toward intelligence. With the political need for a "peace dividend" acutely felt, Congress and the White House oversaw a gradual decline in real defense spending that affected the Intelligence Community as well. Declining defense budgets soon meant relatively declining intelligence budgets, which in turn put a premium on cost-cutting, consolidation and efficiency. Similar concerns had surfaced during the debate over the creation of CIA (when demobilization, not the incipient Cold War, was still the primary consideration in defense budgeting).[22] To many members of Congress in 1992—as in 1947—the answer seemed to lie in increased authority for the DCI, who in turn could motivate a leaner, more agile Intelligence Community.

Congress in the 1990s partially supplanted E.O. 12333 with a series of amendments to the National Security Act. Those amendments were occasionally proscriptive (like the prohibitions added in the 1980s), but often they mandated various acts by the DCI. The intelligence-related passages of the National Security Act—which had hardly been amended at all before 1980—grew from 22 pages of text in the 1990 edition of the House Permanent Select Committee on Intelligence's *Compilation of Intelligence Laws* to 48 pages in the 2000 version.[23]

---

[21] Robert M. Gates, "The CIA and American Foreign Policy," *Foreign Affairs* 66 (Winter 1987/88), p. 225.
[22] Rhodri Jeffreys-Jones, "Why Was the CIA Established in 1947?," *Intelligence and National Security* 12 (January 1997), p. 30.
[23] Unless otherwise noted, all amendments to the National Security Act cited herein are published in the several editions (1993, 1998, or 2000) of the House Permanent Select Committee on Intelligence's *Compilation of Intelligence Laws.*

Foremost among these amendments was the Intelligence Organization Act of 1992.[24] Inspired by the reforms of the Joint Chiefs of Staff accomplished in the 1986 Goldwater-Nichols Act, the legislation—for the first time in a statute—specified the roles (as opposed to the duties) of the Director of Central Intelligence.[25] The DCI was to serve as head of the Intelligence Community, as principal intelligence adviser to the president, and as head of the CIA. As principal intelligence adviser he was to provide the nation's senior policymakers, commanders, and lawmakers with "national" intelligence that was "timely, objective, independent of political considerations, and based on all sources." As head of the Agency he was to collect and evaluate intelligence (particularly from human sources), and to perform services of common concern and "such other functions and duties" as had been suggested since 1947. As head of the Intelligence Community he was to develop the Community's budget, to advise the Secretary of Defense in the appointments of chiefs for the military's joint intelligence agencies, to set collection requirements and priorities, to eliminate unneeded duplication, and to coordinate the community's relationships with foreign intelligence services.

The Intelligence Organization Act also codified the DCI's budgetary powers as described in E.O. 12333, considerably strengthening their provisions. The act decreed that the budgets of the various components of the Intelligence Community could not be incorporated into the annual National Foreign Intelligence Program until approved by the DCI, and required all agencies to obtain DCI approval before reprogramming any NFIP funds. In addition, the Act gave the Director something new: a carefully limited authority to shift funds and personnel from one NFIP project to another (provided he obtained approvals from the White House, Congress, and the affected agency's head).

Events at mid-decade lent new urgency to the unfinished task of modernizing the Intelligence Community. At CIA, the arrest of Aldrich Ames and the spy scandal that ensued led to bipartisan calls for reform of the Agency. The subsequent Republican takeover of Congress in the 1994 elections seemed to provide an opportunity for sweeping changes in the community as a whole. Finally, the re-ordering of national priorities after the end of the Cold War had meant substantial budget cuts for the US

---

[24] The Intelligence Organization Act was passed as part of the Intelligence Authorization Act for FY 1993. Much of its text came from S. 2198, introduced by Sen. David L. Boren (D-OK) and titled the "Intelligence Reorganization Act of 1992." S. 2198 proposed a "Director of National Intelligence" to head the Intelligence Community; subordinate to this new officer would be the newly-styled "Director of the Central Intelligence Agency." Senate Select Committee on Intelligence, "S. 2198 and S. 421 to Reorganize the United States Intelligence Community," 102d Congress, 2d Session, 1992, p. 2. The companion bill in the House of Representatives was HR. 4165, which offered a milder version of the DNI proposal. See also Frank J. Smist, Jr., *Congress Oversees the United States Intelligence Community, 1947-1994* (Knoxville: University of Tennessee Press, 1994 [2d ed.]), pp. 286-287.

[25] The Goldwater-Nichols Act is widely credited with adding coherence to the Joint Chiefs of Staff structure—another creation of the National Security Act of 1947—which had long been viewed as fragmented and less effective than it should have been in advising the commander-in-chief. Among other reforms, Goldwater-Nichols strengthened the Chairman of the Joint Chiefs, naming him (as opposed to the Joint Chiefs as a body) the principal military adviser to the President, clarifying his place in the national chain of command, giving him a Vice Chairman and improving the Joint Staff. See Ronald H. Cole et al., *The Chairmanship of the Joint Chiefs of Staff* (Washington: Office of the Chairman of the Joint Chiefs of Staff [Joint History Office], 1995), pp. 25-38.

military, resulting in reduced budgets and lower personnel ceilings for the Intelligence Community.[26] While military and intelligence resources had been reduced in early 1990s, however, Washington committed American forces to several, major overseas deployments in Africa, the Balkans, the Middle East and the Caribbean.

The White House responded to the new situation by re-ordering intelligence priorities. The burgeoning military deployments demanded ever more tactical intelligence support, and President William Clinton issued a 1995 presidential order (PDD-35) instructing the Intelligence Community to provide it. Explaining his directive at CIA headquarters a few months later, he emphasized that the Community's first priority was to support "the intelligence needs of our military during an operation." Commanders in the field needed "prompt, thorough intelligence to fully inform their decisions and maximize the security of our troops."[27] Since the military spent most of the 1990s deployed in one peacekeeping operation after another (often with more than one taking place at a time), the result of the commitment in PDD-35 was a diversion of shrinking national, strategic intelligence resources to growing, tactical missions.

Congress took a little longer to respond. In 1995 Congressional and outside critics coalesced in no fewer than six separate panels to study the US intelligence effort and recommend reforms.[28] Almost all of the reports published by these groups endorsed a greater degree of centralization and enhanced authority for the Director of Central Intelligence.[29] The wide variance in the size and scope of the study groups—which

---

[26] Commission on National Security/21st Century, *Road Map for National Security: Imperative for Change* (Washington: United States Government Printing Office, 2001), p. 82.

[27] President William J. Clinton, address to the US Intelligence Community, delivered at the Central Intelligence Agency's headquarters, 14 July 1995.

[28] The six panels' reports were: Commission on the Roles and Missions of the United States Intelligence Community [the Brown-Aspin commission], *Preparing for the 21st Century: An Appraisal of US Intelligence* (Washington: United States Government Printing Office, 1996); House Permanent Select Committee on Intelligence, "IC21: Intelligence Community in the 21st Century," 104th Cong., 2d Sess., 1996; Richard N. Haass, Project Director for the Independent Task Force, *Making Intelligence Smarter: The Future of US Intelligence* (New York: Council on Foreign Relations, 1996); Working Group on Intelligence Reform [Abram Shulsky and Gary Schmitt, authors], *The Future of US Intelligence* (Washington: Consortium for the Study of Intelligence, 1996); the Twentieth Century Fund Task Force on the Future of US Intelligence [Stephen Bosworth, chairman], *In From the Cold* (New York: Twentieth Century Fund Press, 1996), and Georgetown University's Institute for the Study of Diplomacy [John Hollister Hedley, author], *Checklist for the Future of Intelligence* (Washington: Institute for the Study of Diplomacy, 1995).

[29] The lone dissenter was the Consortium for the Study of Intelligence's report, overseen by Georgetown political scientist Roy Godson and Harvard historian Ernest May. Its authors concluded:
> . . .the failure of centralization efforts can be seen as reflecting the reasonable needs of the various components of the national security bureaucracy. In any case, the centralized model was probably better suited to the Cold War, with its emphasis on "national" level intelligence about the Soviet strategic nuclear threat, than to the present period when departmental, regional, and tactical intelligence requirements have exploded and gained new urgency. [See pp. xiv-xv.]

ranged in stature from academic colloquia to the presidentially-appointed "Brown-Aspin" commission—seemed to highlight their basic agreement on this issue. The Brown-Aspin commission report perhaps expressed the feeling best. After considering arguments for decentralization, the report cited President Truman's disgust with the bureaucratic rivalry that "contributed to the disaster at Pearl Harbor" and concluded that "returning to a more decentralized system would be a step in the wrong direction." The report declined to suggest alterations in "the fundamental relationship between the DCI and the Secretary of Defense," but nonetheless urged a strengthening of "the DCI's ability to provide centralized management of the Intelligence Community."[30]

Congress heeded the conclusions and the recommendations of these several reports when it drafted the Intelligence Renewal and Reform Act of 1996. That Act, among its other provisions, required the Secretary of Defense to win the concurrence of the DCI in appointing directors for the National Security Agency, the new National Imagery and Mapping Agency, and the National Reconnaissance Office. Under the Act, the DCI would also write (for the NSC) annual performance appraisals of these three agencies.[31] The Act also gave the DCI several new aides (nominated by the President and confirmed by the Senate) to assist in managing the Intelligence Community: a Deputy Director of Central Intelligence for Community Management, as well as Assistant Directors of Central Intelligence for Collection, Analysis and Production, and Administration. It also enhanced the DCI's role as an adviser to the Pentagon's tactical and inter-service intelligence programs, strengthened his limited ability to "reprogram" money and personnel between national intelligence programs and created a sub-committee of the NSC to establish annual priorities for the Intelligence Community.

Congress did not, however, resist the shift of national means to tactical ends. The shift of intelligence resources toward support for military operations worried officials and observers of the Intelligence Community. Indeed, DCI Robert Gates complained as early as 1992 that cuts in the defense budget were forcing the military to trim tactical intelligence programs and pass their work on to the "national" intelligence services.[32] PDD-35 seemed to make the situation even more acute. More than one appraisal in the year after its issuance warned that "support to the warfighter" could demand a disproportionate share of intelligence efforts; a Congressional study even blamed PDD-35, in part, for this development.[33] Nevertheless, these worries remained on the margins of the debate for several more years.

The Twentieth Century Fund's report did not discuss the DCI's responsibilities or the centralization issue, although a "Background Paper" by Allan E. Goodman (bound with the report) implicitly endorsed greater powers for the DCI; see p. 78.

[30] Commission on Roles and Missions, *Preparing for the 21st Century*, pp. xix, 51-52.

[31] See Sections 808 and 815 of the Intelligence Authorization Act for Fiscal Year 1997; *Compilation of Intelligence Laws* (1998).

[32] Testimony of Robert Gates on 1 April 1992 at the Joint Hearing, Senate Select Committee on Intelligence and House Permanent Select Committee on Intelligence, "S. 2198 and S. 421 to Reorganize the United States Intelligence Community," 102nd Cong., 2nd Sess., 1992, p. 108.

[33] For expressions of official and outside concern, see House Permanent Select Committee on Intelligence, "IC21: Intelligence Community in the 21st Century," 104th Cong., 2d Sess., 1996, p. 245. See also the joint comment by Morton I. Abramowitz and Richard Kerr in Richard N. Haass, Project Director for the

Contradictory Impulses

The net effect of the changes made both by the White House and by Congress under both Republican and Democratic majorities was to urge the DCI to exercise more control over the Intelligence Community while limiting his freedom to allocate "national" intelligence resources among competing priorities. Members of Congress collectively seemed impatient with executive branch implementation of reforms to streamline and motivate the community during a long decade of shrinking real defense budgets. At the same time, however, no Congress seriously considered forcing the various civilian and military agencies into a unitary system with a Director of Central Intelligence (or whatever the title) transformed into a true intelligence czar. The executive branch neither assisted nor resisted this congressional impulse to enhance the DCI's authority and the centralization of the Intelligence Community. In effect, however, the White House's aforementioned actions with regard to intelligence were anything but neutral.

The contradictory impulses affecting the Intelligence Community showed in the way the executive and legislative branches together crafted a 1996 law, the National Imagery and Mapping Agency (NIMA) Act, which created the Department of Defense agency of that name out of components from CIA and Defense. While this marked a diminution of the DCI's direct control over imagery analysis, the NIMA Act took pains to preserve DCI authority to prioritize assignments for "national imagery collection assets" and to resolve conflicts among competing priorities.[34] The net effect was ambiguous; the DCI and the CIA lost actual, day-to-day control over an important component of the Intelligence Community, but gained a statutory voice in the nation's employment of that component.

In 1998 DCI George Tenet issued a reconstituted series of Director of Central Intelligence Directives (DCIDs), led by a new DCID-1/1, titled "The Authorities and Responsibilities of the Director of Central Intelligence as Head of the US Intelligence Community." DCIDs had traditionally not been issued as policy statements; they had essentially been implementing documents for the policies established in the NSCIDs (and later in the executive orders). DCID 1/1 stayed well within this tradition, but provided an important reference for the entire community by arranging and citing in one document the key passages of Executive Order 12333 and the amended National Security Act.

The preface to DCID 1/1 stated that it was only intended to be "illustrative." Indeed, readers were directed to the citations "for controlling language." This spare format perhaps conveyed a message more powerful than its authors realized. The DCI's new-found ability to cite so many passages of the United States Code to buttress his authority meant that his powers had grown substantially since its meager beginnings in

---

Independent Task Force, *Making Intelligence Smarter: The Future of US Intelligence* (New York: Council on Foreign Relations, 1996), p. 38.

[34] See Section 1112 of the National Imagery and Mapping Agency Act, which was passed as part of the National Defense Authorization Act for Fiscal Year 1997; *Compilation of Intelligence Laws* (2000).

January 1946. The fact that a DCI felt the need to cite all those passages for the edification of Intelligence Community colleagues, however, suggests that his authority still had far to go.

The blurring of the divide between "national" and "tactical" intelligence seemed at decade's end to provide unclear portents for the future of the DCI's authority. By 2000 the earlier warnings were widely seen to have been accurate. A high-level study commission recently has complained that declining intelligence resources, combined with increased demands for "warning and crisis management," have resulted in:

> . . .an Intelligence Community that is more demand-driven. . . . . That demand is also more driven by military consumers and, therefore, what the Intelligence Community is doing is narrower and more short-term than it was two decades ago.[35]

Another commission, reporting its findings on the National Reconnaissance Office, found in PDD-35 a lightning rod for its criticism:

> There appears to be no effective mechanism to alert policy-makers to the negative impact on strategic requirements that may result from strict adherence to the current Presidential Decision Directive (PDD-35) assigning top priority to military force protection. That Directive has not been reviewed recently to determine whether it has been properly applied and should remain in effect.[36]

The Elusive Vision of Central Intelligence

> Today, intelligence remains the only area of highly complex government activity where overall management across departmental and agency lines is seriously attempted.[37]

Ten years past the end of the Cold War and five since the spate of reform proposals in 1996, this observation by the Brown-Aspin commission seems to remain valid. The Director of Central Intelligence is nominally stronger now; new laws and amendments have augmented his power to lead the Intelligence Community. Nevertheless, the community remains a confederated system, in which the DCI has leadership responsibilities greater than his responsibilities. The system seems roughly balanced between the need for central direction and the imperative to preserve departmental intelligence autonomy. If that balance perhaps appears to be less than optimal, there nevertheless is no obvious imperative to correct it in any fundamental way. Indeed, the 2001 report of the blue-ribbon "Commission on National Security/21st

---

[35] Commission on National Security, *Road Map for National Security*, p. 82.

[36] National Commission for the Review of the National Reconnaissance Office, Final Report (Washington: United States Government Printing Office, 2000), p. 51.

[37] Commission on Roles and Missions, *Preparing for the 21st Century*, p. 47.

Century" (the Hart-Rudman commission) recommended "no major structural changes" in the management of the Intelligence Community and noted that "current efforts to strengthen community management while maintaining the ongoing relationship between the DCI and the Secretary of Defense are bearing fruit."[38]

The members of Congress who passed the National Security Act of 1947 had wanted the new Central Intelligence Agency to provide policymakers the best possible information and to coordinate clandestine operations. They assumed that the President's intelligence officer—the Director of Central Intelligence—would accomplish these objectives, and left the executive branch to its own initiative for the next four decades. This was how Congress resolved the dilemma of having a "national" intelligence system that was not centrally controlled. Succeeding presidents oversaw the Intelligence Community through a series of National Security Council Intelligence Directives and executive orders, which recognized the gap between coordination and control and encouraged DCIs to do more to bridge it and to manage America's intelligence efforts. After the Cold War ended, however, Democratic and Republican Congresses grew impatient with the executive branch and urged that intelligence be done centrally. Nonetheless, no Congress grasped the nettle of sweeping reform, either to decentralize the system or to give the DCI command authority over military intelligence and the departmental intelligence offices. At the same time, the executive branch's insistence on using declining resources first and foremost to support military operations effectively blunted the Congressional emphasis on centralization by limiting the wherewithal that DCIs and agency heads could devote to national and strategic objectives.

This ambiguity is likely to endure for the same reasons it arose in the first place: no one can agree on what should replace it. Reform faces the same obstacles that Harry Truman and his aides encountered in 1945. Everyone has a notion of how reform should be implemented, but everyone also has a specific list of changes they will not tolerate. The mix of preferences and objections produces a veto to almost every proposal, until the one that survives is the one policymakers and legislators dislike the least. Ambiguity is also likely to keep alive the durable idea—born from the Pearl Harbor disaster—that the axiomatic principles of unity of command and unity of intelligence can best be served through an increased centralization of US intelligence efforts.

America's national security framework forces such ambiguities on policymakers and commanders for good reasons as well as bad. The great economic and military strength of America and the comparative material wealth of its Intelligence Community has provided a certain latitude for experimentation—and even duplication of effort—in the service of higher, political goals. In such a context, a decentralized Intelligence Community may be the only kind of system that can maintain public and military support for an independent, civilian foreign intelligence arm in America's non-parliamentary form of government, where it is possible for the two major political parties to split control over the executive and legislative branches of government. Decentralization assures the Pentagon of military control over its tactical and joint intelligence programs. It also

---

[38] Commission on National Security, *Road Map for National Security*, p. 83.

assures members of Congress of both parties that the President's chief intelligence adviser cannot acquire a dangerous concentration of domestic political power or monopolize the foreign policy advice flowing into the White House. Thus we are likely to live with the de-centralized intelligence system—and the impulse toward centralization—until a crisis re-aligns the political and bureaucratic players or compels them to cooperate in new ways.